Testimonials

"Being around the "Triple Spirals" means that your day is likely to be punctuated, seemingly at random, by chant and song. The Triple Spirals use vocal music in the old way: for bonding the community, for communicating shared experience, for creating a participatory sound with which you are invited to join, for creating fun, for moving the human soul. There is also the more obvious focus of the Triple Spiral chants: the text itself. But rather like The Form in Tai Chi, the text of the chant is to give your brain something to occupy it while your body and soul are chanting."

~ **Scot AnSgeulaiche**, Scottish Tradition Keeper

"What I love most about these entrancing Triple Spiral chants are their beauty and the ease of their simplicity. One can learn them quickly to sing alone or with others for a myriad of sacred purposes. The melodies and evocative lyrics enhance any spiritual gathering or ritual."

~ **Rev. Judith Laxer**, founder of Gaia's Temple and MoonWise Mystery School

"Gina Martin and her choir and music weaves such a diverse collection of people together."

~ **Laney Goodman**, Drummer and National Syndicated Radio Host of *Women in Music*

"Traditional, mystical, and original tunes of praise and promise.
A blend of women's skills, passions, purpose set to music; to enchant, invoke and invite.
Elemental invocations, translations, salutations, and prayers – simple and profound.
Calling forth the Goddess in her many guises.
Casting spells, telling tales, welcoming power and grace to the circle.
The wheel turns. Earth, water, fire, air, center.
SHE hears the wise women singing and awakens."

~ **Mosa Baczewska**, Digital Painter, Songwriter, Jill Love All Trades

WomEnchanting

WomEnchanting

Gina Martin

ACADEMY PRESS

Copyright © 2021 Gina Martin. All rights reserved.

No part of this publication shall be reproduced, transmitted, or sold in whole or in part in any form without prior written consent of the author, except as provided by the United States of America copyright law. Any unauthorized usage of the text without express written permission of the publisher is a violation of the author's copyright and is illegal and punishable by law. All trademarks and registered trademarks appearing in this guide are the property of their respective owners.

For permission requests, write to the below address:

PYP Academy Press
141 Weston Street, #155
Hartford, CT 06141

The opinions expressed by the Author are not necessarily those held by PYP Academy Press.

Ordering Information: Quantity sales and special discounts are available on quantity purchases by corporations, associations, and others. For details, contact the author at www.triplespiralofdunnasidhe.net/contact.

Edited by: Emily Ribiero
Cover design by: Cornelia Murariu
Typeset by: Medlar Publishing Solutions Pvt Ltd., India

Printed in the United States of America.

ISBN: 978-1-955985-04-8 (paperback)

Library of Congress Control Number: 20219117418

First edition, October 2021

The information contained within this book is strictly for informational purposes. The material may include information, products, or services by third parties. As such, the Author and Publisher do not assume responsibility or liability for any third-party material or opinions. The publisher is not responsible for websites (or their content) that are not owned by the publisher. Readers are advised to do their own due diligence when it comes to making decisions.

The mission of the Publish Your Purpose Academy Press is to discover and publish authors who are striving to make a difference in the world. We give underrepresented voices power and a stage to share their stories, speak their truth, and impact their communities. Do you have a book idea you would like us to consider publishing? Please visit PublishYourPurposePress.com for more information.

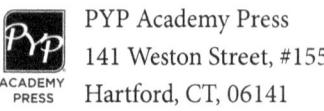

PYP Academy Press
141 Weston Street, #155
Hartford, CT, 06141

Contents

Preface . . . . *xi*
How to Use this Book . . . . *xiii*
Categories for Usage . . . . *xv*

Casting of Community – the Óenach 1
All Will Be Well 3
Artemis 5
Begin Again 7
Breathe 9
Bridget Invocation 11
Cailleach 13
Call in the Directions 15
A Circle of Women 17
Come Light the Fire Now 19
Danu Chant 21
Dark Dark Green 23
Dark is the Night 25
Domnu 27
Fire, Fire 29
For the Great Queen 31
Hecate's Song 33
Howl 35

Hymn to the Great Mother	36
I Am Free	39
Iamenja	41
Inanna	43
Isis	45
Kali Ma	47
Kostroma Temple Dance	49
Lee's Song	51
Lullaby	53
Maiden Song	55
The Menstruatin' Maiden Blues	56
Mokosh	59
Morrigan Invocation	61
Prayer of Strength	63
Priestess Song	65
Rhiannon	67
Roots	69
Sacred Space	71
Samhain Song	73
Triple Spiral Processional Chant	74
Vessel	77
What Is Divine	79
Women of the Circle	81
Releasing the Community	83

Acknowledgements *84*

Preface

Who are we?
Twenty-two years ago, we held our first Samhain ceremony here at Dún na Sidhe, a sweet parcel of land in the foothills of the Ramapough Mountains in the Hudson Valley. We came together as a spiritual community of folks drawn to Remember, to remember the Old Ways, to honor the earth, to nurture our personal relationships with the Divine, and to find the freedom and joy to speak of the Goddess, She of a Thousand Names openly. Finding our authentic path to the old and the new, we resonate deeply with the divine forces of the Celts, and always open our ceremonies and rituals acknowledging the Native ancestors who stewarded this land before us, the Ramapough Lenape. While we adhere to no specific tradition we learn from all and respectfully incorporate the wisdoms of many.

And we sing. A lot. The songs and chants in this book have been written by the women and girls of Triple Spiral. They lift our hearts—and we hope they will serve to do that for you too. We sing through laughter and tears as we call the Goddess to be present in our lives.

We first started meeting at Full Moons to give women and girls a safe place to connect with the Goddess. We have held First Moon rituals, Mothering ceremonies, Croning rituals and facilitated two groups of Priestesses through their training. Until Covid brought the world to a halt we had held Full Moon rituals continuously for twenty years.

Almost immediately we saw that the path for this healing connection to Her was needed by our sons and partners as well. Over the years we have held community ceremonies at the Fire Feasts, pre-dawn hikes up the local mountain for Equinoxes and Solstices for the boys, and special coming of age ceremonies for the young men among us. Our goal is to manifest healing though balance, and to nourish our connection to All That Is.

We formed our not-for-profit congregation over ten years ago as a step toward protecting the community and the land. All the profits from this book and these recordings will go directly to Triple Spiral of Dún na Sidhe to help maintain the land, build a classroom, and to foster programs for teaching meaningful ethics and practices for our families, our communities, our Earth, and our connection to the Divine.

In Her service,
Gina Martin, High Priestess of Triple Spiral of Dún na Sidhe

How to Use this Book

Within these pages are the sounds of women singing in the moonlight, the sounds of women and men, girls and boys singing to the Samhain Fire, the sound of a person singing another to their rest—the music from our hearts that has given us deep meaning and a source of profound healing.

We've divided our songs and chants into six categories: music to honor the Elements, the Seasons, the Cycles of life, to raise and to ground energy, and to praise specific Goddesses. However, most of these pieces have multiple uses. For example, the *Brighid Invocation* is a summons to the Goddess Brighid and can also be used at Imbolc to celebrate that Fire Feast in the Turning of the Wheel. The *Fire Fire* chant is a paean to the Element as well as a powerful energy raiser.

These categories are merely suggestions of when specific songs and chants might be useful to you in your communities and/or solitary practices. But, as always, the heart knows what the heart knows, so we encourage you to make use of these tools however feels best to you. The songs and chants were written to be responsive to the energy of the Circle. Some can be sung as rounds, others with one verse as melody and the other as descant. Our recordings can give you a good idea of how the music can swell and build and evolve into what needs to be, and we offer you a free download of one chant to get a feel of what is possible. Go to https://www.triplespiralofdunnasidhe.net/purchase-music to purchase the recordings individually as you wish.

We offer this book to you for your greatest good and wish you joy and bright blessings.

In Her service,
Gina Martin

Categories for Usage

Elemental: Breathe, Fire Fire, For the Great Queen, Isis, Prayer of Strength, Roots, Sacred Space

Seasonal: Come Light the Fire Now, For the Great Queen, Kostroma Temple Dance, Samhain Song

Cycles: Begin Again, Breathe, Come Light the Fire Now, Kostroma Temple Dance, Lee's Song, Maiden Song, Triple Spiral Processional Chant, Women of the Circle

Raising Energy: Artemis, Cailleach, A Circle of Women, Danu, Dark Dark Green, Dark Is the Night, Fire Fire, Howl, I am Free, Iamenja, Inanna, Kali Ma, Morrigan Invocation, Priestess Song Sacred Space, Triple Spiral Processional Chant, Vessel, What is Divine

Grounding Energy: All Will be Well, Begin Again, Call in Directions, Casting of Community, Releasing the Community, Dark Dark Green, Inanna, Isis, Lullaby, Roots, What is Divine

Goddess: Artemis, Bridget Invocation, Cailleach, Danu, Dark Dark Green, Domnu, For the Great Queen, Hecate's Song, Hymn to the Great Mother, Iamenja, Inanna, Isis, Kali Ma, Kostroma Temple Dance, Mokosh, Morrigan Invocation, Rhiannon

Casting of Community – the Óenach

Lyrics and Melody by Sharynne NicMhacha

Rom   chri - de - ón   is   mo   che - nón

Translation: Welcome to my heart
Pronunciation: Rove chrith-e-on is mo che-non

Rom as in rove
chritheon
Is as in sit
Mo with the short 'o'
Chenon with ch like loch and the soft 'e' like egg

To purchase this song visit https://www.triplespiralofdunnasidhe.net/purchase-music.
All proceeds go to Triple Spiral of Dún na Sidhe, a not for profit congregation.

All Will Be Well

Lyrics by Julian of Norwich
Melody by Gina Martin

To purchase this song visit https://www.triplespiralofdunnasidhe.net/purchase-music.
All proceeds go to Triple Spiral of Dún na Sidhe, a not for profit congregation.

Artemis

Lyrics and Melody by Gina Martin

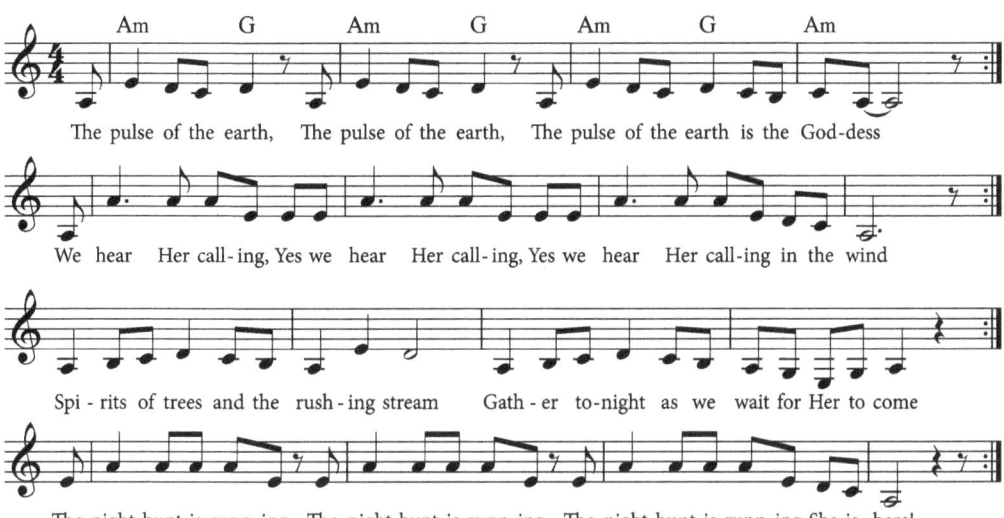

The pulse of the earth, The pulse of the earth, The pulse of the earth is the God-dess
We hear Her call-ing, Yes we hear Her call-ing, Yes we hear Her call-ing in the wind
Spi-rits of trees and the rush-ing stream Gath-er to-night as we wait for Her to come
The night hunt is runn-ing The night hunt is runn-ing The night hunt is runn-ing She is here!

Begin Again

Lyrics Traditional
Melody by Gina Martin

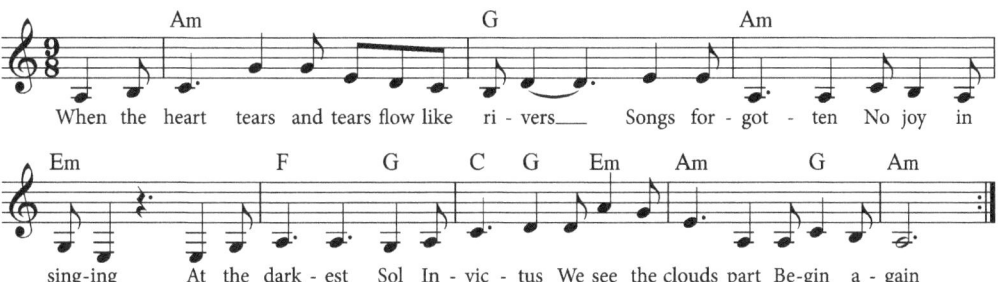

Verse II
When we struggle
And tides pull us backward
When Life's weight is
Beyond bearing
At the darkest
Sol Invictus
We see the clouds part
Begin Again

Verse III
When we call the
Sun and the Moonlight
When we stand in the Sacred
Circle
There is strength when
Hands are clasping
We see the clouds part
Begin Again

To purchase this song visit https://www.triplespiralofdunnasidhe.net/purchase-music.
All proceeds go to Triple Spiral of Dún na Sidhe, a not for profit congregation.

Breathe

Lyrics by Laura Delano
Melody by Gina Martin

Air is here
So plant your seed
Air is here
Bring forth your dream

Breathe in the new
Breathe out the old
Breathe in the warmth
Release the cold
And Breathe, Breathe, Breathe

Bridget Invocation

Lyrics and Melody by Gina Martin
Irish Translation by Anna Kelly

An Mhai-tair Brid Mas e do thoi-le Lig is-teach___ ag-us fail-te rom-hat An Mhai-tair Brid

Pronunciation:
An Ma-her Breej Mash e doe hey-lay Lig ish-tcha___ a-gus falt-cha ro-wit An Ma-her Breej

Translation:
Divine Mother Bridget Please, Come in and be with us, and Welcome

To purchase this song visit https://www.triplespiralofdunnasidhe.net/purchase-music.
All proceeds go to Triple Spiral of Dún na Sidhe, a not for profit congregation.

Cailleach

Lyrics and Melody by Gina Martin

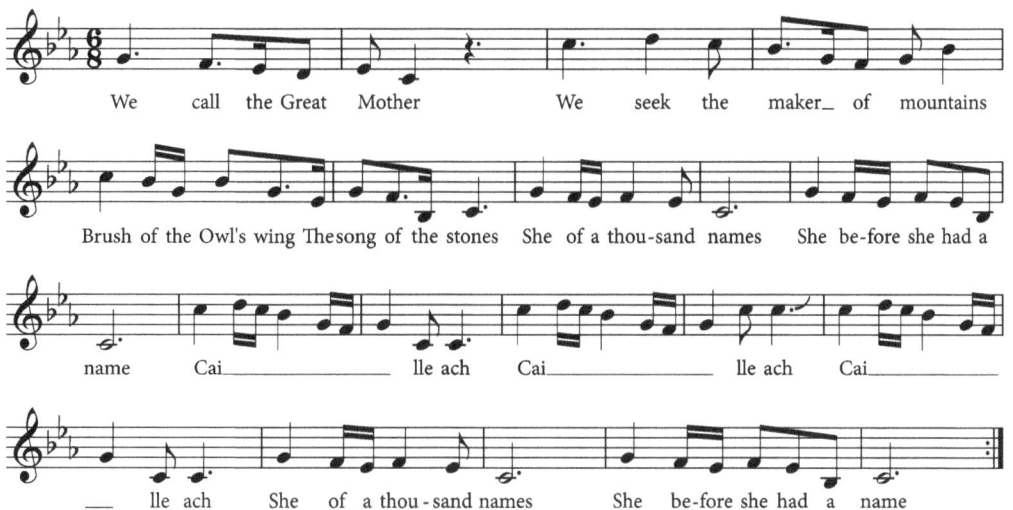

We seek the Great Wisdom
We call the ancestors
forward
Shadows of Women,
The thrum in the bone
She of a thousand names
She before she had a name

Cailleach
Cailleach
Cailleach
She of a thousand names
She before she had a name

To purchase this song visit https://www.triplespiralofdunnasidhe.net/purchase-music.
All proceeds go to Triple Spiral of Dún na Sidhe, a not for profit congregation.

Call in the Directions

Lyrics and Melody by Gina Martin

I call the North, the Mother Earth. I long for Her warm embrace. And from the West the Water flows and blesses this place. The South brings Fire joyful, the East the breath of dawn. The Center holds me sweet and strong. I stand in Sacred Space.

Sunwise

I call the East, the light of dawn, fresh breeze across my face.
And from the South the Fire of joy burns brightly in this place.
The West brings blessed Water,
The North the Mother Earth.
The Center holds me sweet and strong. I stand in Sacred Space.

Triple Spiral of Dún na Sidhe © 2021

A Circle of Women

Lyrics and Melody by Gina Martin

To purchase this song visit https://www.triplespiralofdunnasidhe.net/purchase-music.
All proceeds go to Triple Spiral of Dún na Sidhe, a not for profit congregation.

Come Light the Fire Now

Lyrics and Melody by Gina Martin

To purchase this song visit https://www.triplespiralofdunnasidhe.net/purchase-music.
All proceeds go to Triple Spiral of Dún na Sidhe, a not for profit congregation.

Danu Chant

Lyrics and Melody by Gina Martin

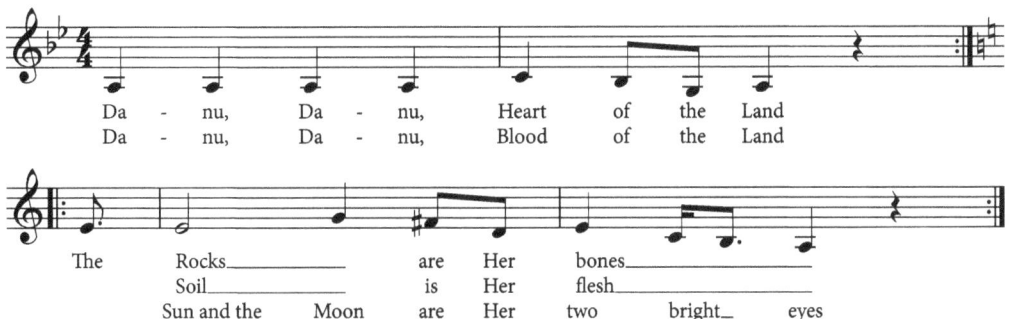

To purchase this song visit https://www.triplespiralofdunnasidhe.net/purchase-music.
All proceeds go to Triple Spiral of Dún na Sidhe, a not for profit congregation.

Dark Dark Green

Lyrics by Laura Delano
Melody by Leonore Tjia

To purchase this song visit https://www.triplespiralofdunnasidhe.net/purchase-music.
All proceeds go to Triple Spiral of Dún na Sidhe, a not for profit congregation.

Dark is the Night

Lyrics and Melody by Gina Martin

Dark is the Night Dark is the For-est Dark Sis-ters ga-ther Wai-ting, Wai-ting

The veil is thin And sha-dows dee pen Wo-men come and lis-ten, li-sten

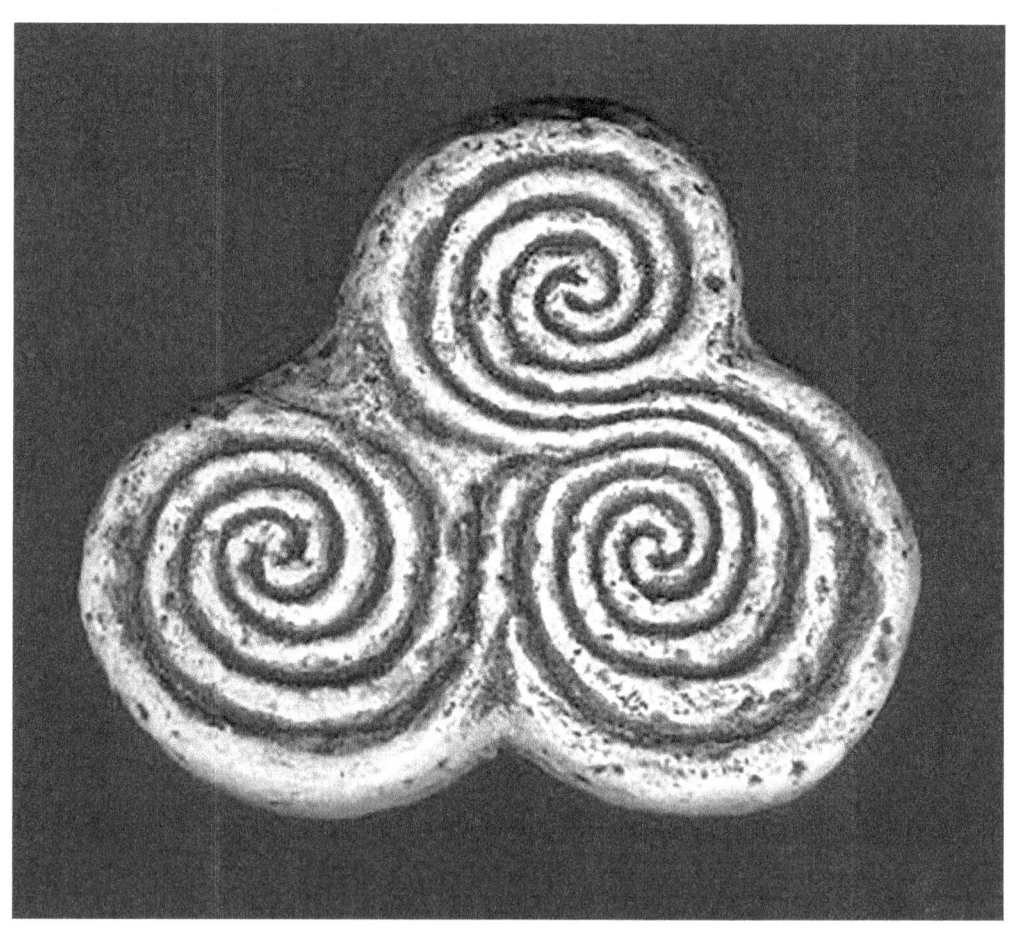

Domnu

Lyrics by Gina Martin
Melody Traditional

To purchase this song visit https://www.triplespiralofdunnasidhe.net/purchase-music.
All proceeds go to Triple Spiral of Dún na Sidhe, a not for profit congregation.

Fire, Fire

Lyrics and Melody by Gina Martin

To purchase this song visit https://www.triplespiralofdunnasidhe.net/purchase-music.
All proceeds go to Triple Spiral of Dún na Sidhe, a not for profit congregation.

For the Great Queen

Lyrics by Gina Martin
Melody Traditional

Triple Spiral of Dún na Sidhe © 2021

Hecate's Song

Lyrics and Melody by Ginny Brooke

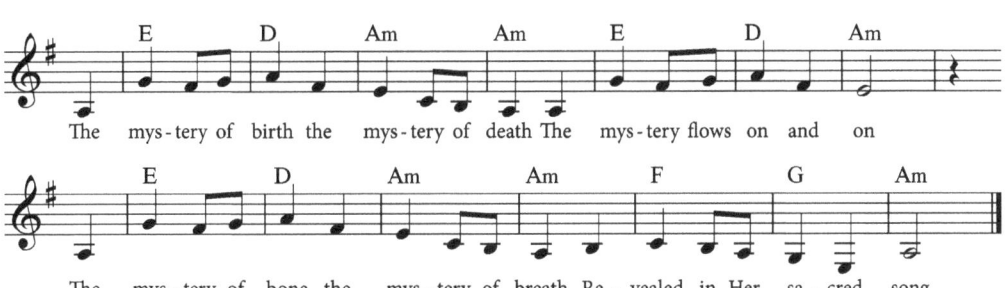

When the light of the moon fills sa-cred space She will come with a torch and sword
And at once you re-mem-ber Her shi-ning face As the One who will cut the cord
The mys-tery of birth the mys-tery of death The mys-tery flows on and on
The mys-tery of bone the mys-tery of breath Re-vealed in Her sa-cred song

Crone Drone

Birth Death Bone Breath

Triple Spiral of Dún na Sidhe © 2021

Howl

Lyrics and Melody by Gina Martin

Hymn to the Great Mother

Lyrics and Melody by Gina Martin

*To purchase this song visit https://www.triplespiralofdunnasidhe.net/purchase-music.
All proceeds go to Triple Spiral of Dún na Sidhe, a not for profit congregation.*

I Am Free

Lyrics and Melody by Gina Martin

To purchase this song visit https://www.triplespiralofdunnasidhe.net/purchase-music.
All proceeds go to Triple Spiral of Dún na Sidhe, a not for profit congregation.

Iamenja

Lyrics by Leonore Tjia and Gina Martin
Melody by Gina Martin

Part III:

Iamenga, ocean's primal power / river bright running /
queen of lotus flower / mist tears falling / blood salt and sour /
rain soft thrumming / mind's inner hour / blood gate opening river queen /
mother of tears / freedom from fear / great sea

Inanna

Lyrics by Marianna Carrol and Gina Martin
Melody by Gina Martin

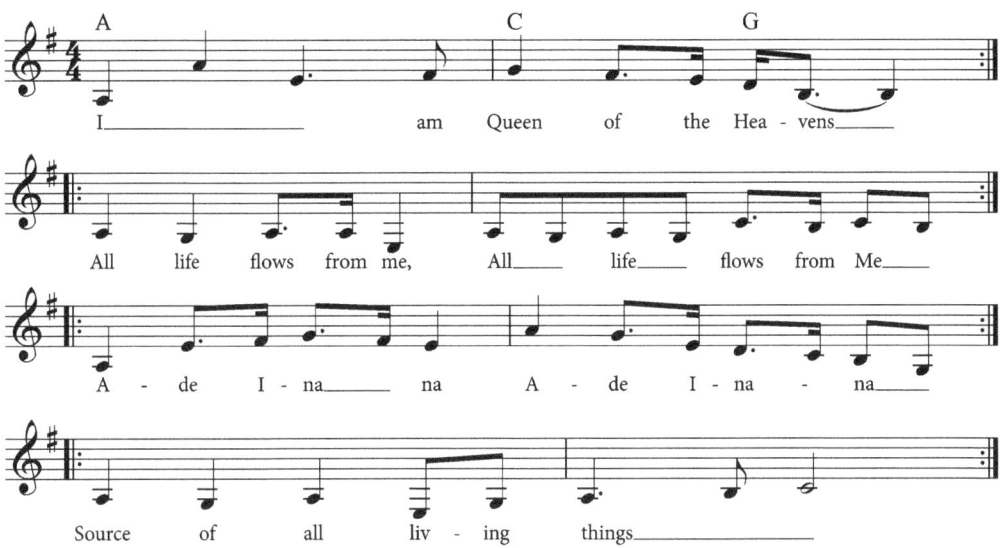

To purchase this song visit https://www.triplespiralofdunnasidhe.net/purchase-music.
All proceeds go to Triple Spiral of Dún na Sidhe, a not for profit congregation.

Isis

Lyrics and Melody by Gina Martin

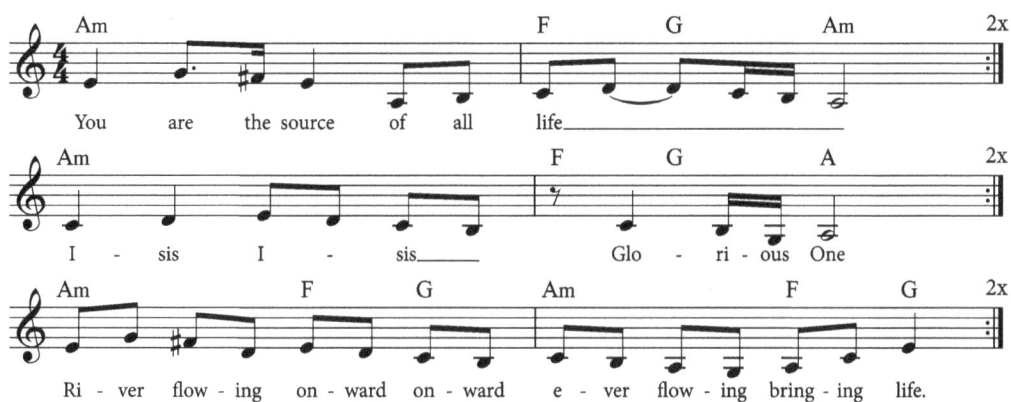

To purchase this song visit *https://www.triplespiralofdunnasidhe.net/purchase-music.*
All proceeds go to Triple Spiral of Dún na Sidhe, a not for profit congregation.

Kali Ma

Lyrics and Melody by Eliza Martin Simpson and Gina Martin

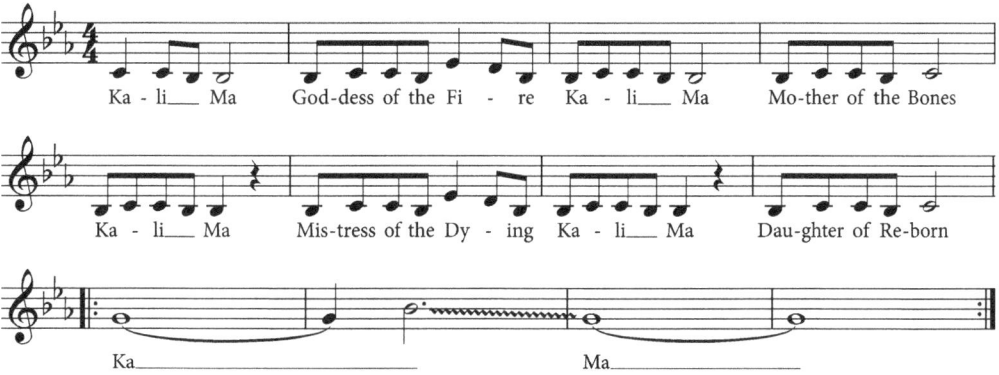

To purchase this song visit https://www.triplespiralofdunnasidhe.net/purchase-music. All proceeds go to Triple Spiral of Dún na Sidhe, a not for profit congregation.

Kostroma Temple Dance

Lyrics by Karen Tarapata
Melody by Gina Martin

In Fall
Death/Life
Dark/Light
Maiden/Mother
Deep Sleep

Triple Spiral of Dún na Sidhe © 2021

Lee's Song

Lyrics and Melody by Gina Martin

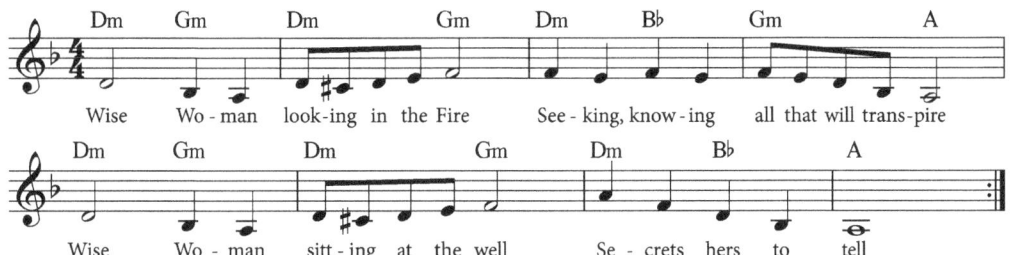

Wise Woman, singing with the Wind
Naming, calling all things to begin

Wise Woman, standing on the Earth
Guiding death and birth

Lullaby

Lyrics by Gina Martin
Melody Traditional

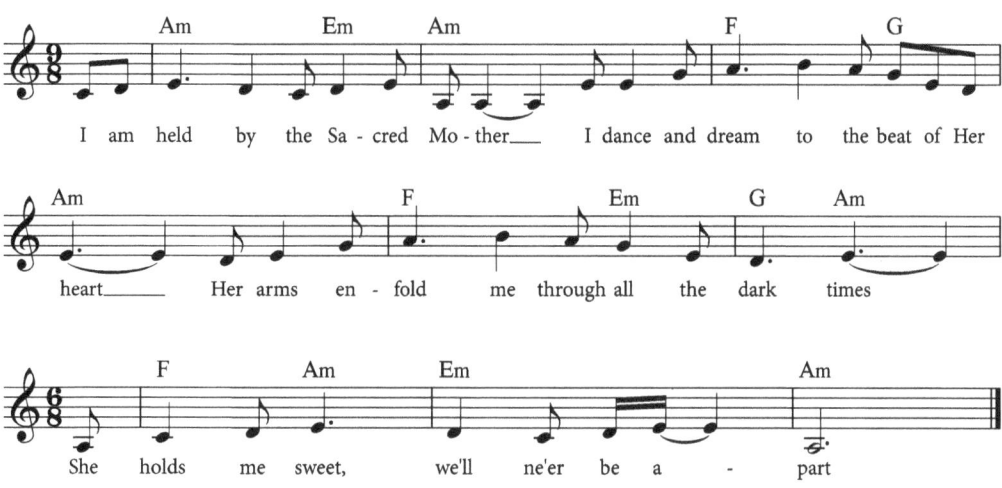

To purchase this song visit https://www.triplespiralofdunnasidhe.net/purchase-music.
All proceeds go to Triple Spiral of Dún na Sidhe, a not for profit congregation.

Maiden Song

Lyrics and Melody by Anna Palmer, Maya Carl, and Gina Martin

*To purchase this song visit https://www.triplespiralofdunnasidhe.net/purchase-music.
All proceeds go to Triple Spiral of Dún na Sidhe, a not for profit congregation.*

The Menstruatin' Maiden Blues

Lyrics and Melody by Ginny Brooke

```
A E                      A E
  Standin' in the grove one night,   full moon on the rise,
A E                     A E
  Called in the directions,   an apparition appeared

  before my eyes.
  A
  She was wearing a skull necklace,   eyes were blazing red,
A E                     A E
  I was feelin' a bit jumpy,   and this is what she said:
  E       B7
  She said, "Leonore and Norma,   I hear you got your moon,
A E                           A E
  Your peaches they are ripening,   they'll be right tasty soon."


  (Chorus)
  B7      A                       E
  O yeah, I got those menstruatin' maiden blues.


A E
  Now that I got your attention
A E
  You best listen to me
A E
  The boys are getting hungry
A E
  They're gonna start shakin your tree
  A
  They tell you they love you
  A
  Beg and plead with you all night
A E
  Their stomachs they are growling
A E
  Thinking about that first tasty bite


  (Chorus)
  B7      A                       E
  O yeah, I got those menstruatin' maiden blues.
```

To purchase this song visit https://www.triplespiralofdunnasidhe.net/purchase-music.
All proceeds go to Triple Spiral of Dún na Sidhe, a not for profit congregation.

```
A E            A E
Some say I am reckless,   some say I am wild,
A E            A E
I eat boys for breakfast,  if they hurt my child.
A
Them skulls on my necklace,   were bruisin' the fruit.
A E            A E
Guess I lost my temper,   and gave'm the boot.
```

(Chorus)
```
B⁷      A              E
O yeah, I got those menstruatin' maiden blues.
```

```
A E         A E
She left in a hurry,   in a great cloud of smoke,
A E              A E
The maidens they were shaking,   they knew it was no joke.
A
So you best heed Her warning,   when you pick out your

man.
A E            A E
Best ask her opinion,   when you fasten your hand.
B⁷
Better make sure he's faithful,   honest and true,
A E              A E
Cause if he ain't, child,   She'll be wearing him too.
```

(Chorus)
```
B⁷     A                   E
O yeah, I got those menstruatin' maiden blues.
```

Mokosh

Lyrics by Karen Tarapata and Gina Martin
Melody by Gina Martin

To purchase this song visit https://www.triplespiralofdunnasidhe.net/purchase-music.
All proceeds go to Triple Spiral of Dún na Sidhe, a not for profit congregation.

Morrigan Invocation

Lyrics and Melody by Gina Martin

Lyrics
Gairim Mor Regan,
Saigim a Mor Thea.
Tait Mor regan!
Foilsigid dom!

Translation
I call the Great Queen,
I seek the Great Goddess.
Come Great Queen!
Reveal to me!

Transliteration
Ga-rim More Ree-gan,
Sah gim a More They-a
Tahd More Ree-gan!
Fahl shi gith dohv!

Prayer of Strength

Melody by Gina Martin
Translation by Sharynne Nic Macha

Today I go forth with
The strength of the Skies,
The brightness of the Sun,
The splendour of the Moon,
The brilliance of Fire,
The swiftness of Lightning,
The speed of the Wind,
The depths of the Sea,
The steadfastness of the earth,
And the steadiness of Rock.

A-dom ryoog in dyoo
Nyurt ni-vuh
Sahlshe ghray-nuh
Ay-troch-tuh aysh-kuh
Ay-troch-tuh aysh-kuh
Aiy-nuh then-eth
Day-nug low-chet
Loo-ah thuh goy-e-thuh
Foo-dohv-nuh vah-roe
Tah-rish-mih-guh thal-vahn
Covsah-thun ah/ih-lech

To purchase this song visit https://www.triplespiralofdunnasidhe.net/purchase-music.
All proceeds go to Triple Spiral of Dún na Sidhe, a not for profit congregation.

Priestess Song

Lyrics and Melody by Gina Martin

To purchase this song visit https://www.triplespiralofdunnasidhe.net/purchase-music.
All proceeds go to Triple Spiral of Dún na Sidhe, a not for profit congregation.

Rhiannon

Lyrics and Melody by Gina Martin

Verse II
Great Queen, Sea foam
Eyes like starlight
Rigatona Rhiannon
Rides the Wind
With silver hoofbeats
Rigatona Rhiannon

Verse III
Horse to bird
To woman shifting
Rigatona Rhiannon
Pulls the tides
With magic music
Rigatona Rhannion

Roots

Lyrics and Melody by Eliza Martin Simpson

To purchase this song visit https://www.triplespiralofdunnasidhe.net/purchase-music.
All proceeds go to Triple Spiral of Dún na Sidhe, a not for profit congregation.

Sacred Space

Lyrics and Melody by Gina Martin

Where I stand is sa-cred space. On this Earth, On this Earth.
I am a child of e - ther Made of star - dust Lightn-ing heart-beats
I am of ra-ging ri - vers Moss - y fae - rie
rocks of bones I am I am Here

Triple Spiral of Dún na Sidhe © 2021

Samhain Song

Lyrics and Melody by Gina Martin

When the old year is end-ing and Light be-comes dear We stand in the
As we sing to the Fi - re and look in the flames to see what the

Cir - cle a - gain And we know that the Winds of the win-ter bring
new year brings in

change so we hold on to those we love dear For we trust in the

Cir - cle and the Cen - ter that holds, the Cen - ter that holds us near

To purchase this song visit https://www.triplespiralofdunnasidhe.net/purchase-music.
All proceeds go to Triple Spiral of Dún na Sidhe, a not for profit congregation.

Triple Spiral of Dún na Sidhe © 2021

Triple Spiral Processional Chant

Lyrics and Melody by Gina Martin and Eliza Martin Simpson

To purchase this song visit https://www.triplespiralofdunnasidhe.net/purchase-music.
All proceeds go to Triple Spiral of Dún na Sidhe, a not for profit congregation.

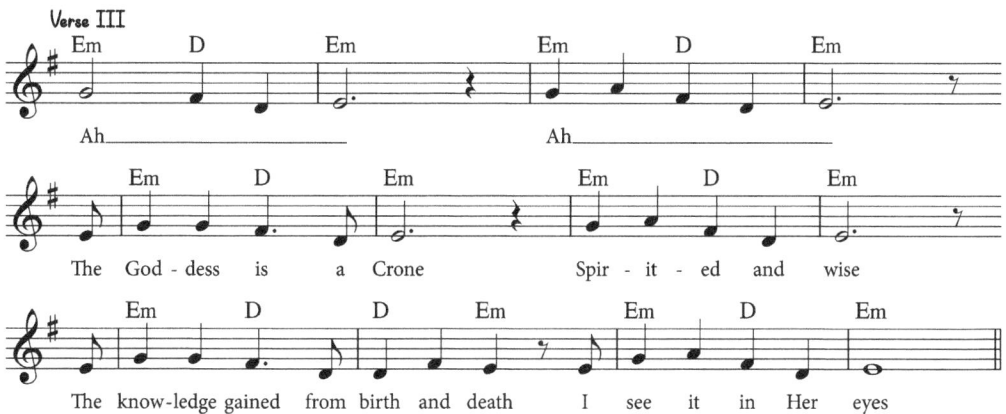

Vessel

Lyrics and Melody by Gina Martin, Kristi Zea and Leonore Tija

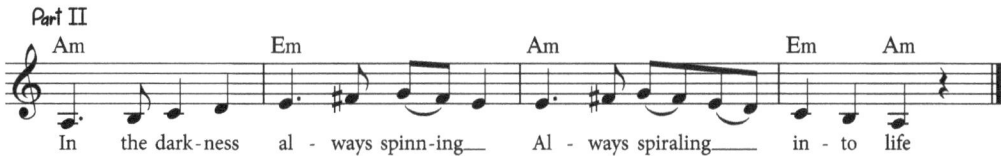

To purchase this song visit https://www.triplespiralofdunnasidhe.net/purchase-music.
All proceeds go to Triple Spiral of Dún na Sidhe, a not for profit congregation.

What Is Divine

Lyrics by Dalia Basiouny and Gina Martin
Melody by Gina Martin

From before time till after time
What is Divine has always been mine
I konw that She can always be found
In temple fine or sacred ground
I call Her name a thousand different ways
And She is here, and here She'll stay

To purchase this song visit https://www.triplespiralofdunnasidhe.net/purchase-music.
All proceeds go to Triple Spiral of Dún na Sidhe, a not for profit congregation.

Women of the Circle

Lyrics and Melody by Gina Martin

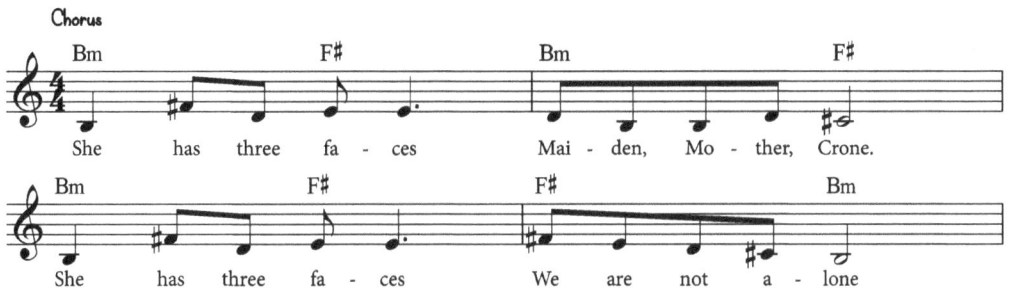

Verse II
Sisters. We turn to our Crones
When troubled in heart
And bound by our fear.
Sisters, we ask for their wisdom
When the path's not clear

Verse III
Sisters, we turn to the Mothers
Looking for comfort,
Arms that enfold, our
Sisters - they hold us so warmly
When our hearts arc cold

Verse IV
Sisters, we turn to our Maidens
Watching them dance and
Feeling them sway.
Sisters, we drink in their laughter
When we've lost our way.

To purchase this song visit https://www.triplespiralofdunnasidhe.net/purchase-music.
All proceeds go to Triple Spiral of Dún na Sidhe, a not for profit congregation.

Releasing the Community

Lyrics and Melody by Gina Martin

A - naid i mo chri - di - u

Translation: Stay/Remain/Abide in my heart
Pronunciation: AH-nidh ih mo CHRIH-dhyoo

Dh represents the 'th' sound as in the words 'the' or 'other'
I'm using 'ih' to represent a short 'i' sound as in 'sit'
Mo has a short 'o' sound as in 'off'
Ch as in 'loch' or 'Bach' (not as in 'choose')

Acknowledgements

So many hours of loving devotion and bountiful laughter with all our creators.

The Music Miracle Making Committee- Ginny Brooke, Gina Martin, and Drucilla Minte Pluhowski
The Millennial Tech Support Angel- Eliza Martin Simpson
The Music App Marvel- Jeremy Straus
The Fabulous Photographers and Artists: Lisa Levart, Hamish Douglas Burgess, Carolina Kroon, Karen Tarapata
The Recording Gurus- Gary Solomon and Barry Carl
The Singers and Musicians- Teagan Heather Blackburn, Ginny Brooke, Liz Carl, Maya Carl, Christina Huber, Quille Hughes, Norma Kuhling, Tracy Louis, Gina Martin, Hilary Okie, Anna Palmer, Maria Palmer, Dru Minte Pluhowski, Eliza Martin Simpson, Karen Tarapata, Leonore Tjia, Bettina Zastrow, Kristi Zea,

And our Proficient Posse of Fabulous Women at Publish Your Purpose Press— Jenn T. Grace and Bailly Morse

Contributors Resource Links:
Gina Martin: www.ginamartinauthor.com www.ginamartinacupuncture.com
Gary Solomon: https://www.facebook.com/Gate-Hill-Audio-214843488555315
Maria Palmer: maria.palmer@mac.com
Lisa Levart: www.GoddessOnEarth.com
Hamish Douglas Burgess: www.mauiceltic.com www.hamishburgess.com.
Carolina Kroon: http://www.carolinakroon.com

Please find us and the links to purchase the recordings at
https://www.triplespiralofdunnasidhe.net/purchase-music

Triple Spiral of Dún na Sidhe- a 501c-3

www.ingramcontent.com/pod-product-compliance
Lightning Source LLC
Chambersburg PA
CBHW061104070526
44579CB00011B/133